THE RISE
OF ISLAM

Peter Chrisp

Themes in History
The American Frontier
The Crusades
The French Revolution and Napoleon
Life in the Middle Ages
The Rise of Islam
The Roman Empire

Cover illustration: Ali, the son-in-law and cousin of Muhammad, was proclaimed caliph, or head of the Islamic community, in 656. In this Persian painting, he receives oaths of loyalty from leading Muslims. The flames that surround him are a sign of holiness in Persian art.

First published in 1991 by
Wayland (Publishers) Limited
61 Western Road, Hove
East Sussex BN3 1JD, England

Series editor: Mike Hirst
Book editor: Rose Hill
Designer: Joyce Chester
Consultant: Dr Charles Melville, lecturer in Middle Eastern
Studies at the University of Cambridge.

British Library Cataloguing in Publication Data
Chrisp, Peter
The Rise of Islam — (Themes in history).
I. Title II. Series
956

ISBN 0 7502 0285 8

Typeset by Dorchester Typesetting Group Ltd
Printed and bound in Italy by
L.E.G.O. S.p.A., Vicenza

Contents

Introduction

At the beginning of the seventh century AD, a new religion appeared in Arabia. Its name was Islam, which means 'giving in to the will of God'. Its followers are called Muslims.

Arabia is a hot, dry region of desert and semi-desert. In the seventh century, most Arabs were nomads, people who live by moving from place to place. These bedouin, as they were called, slept in tents woven from goat hair. They roamed the country with their flocks of sheep, goats and camels, constantly searching for land for fresh grazing. They lived in tribes, which were often at war with one another.

This Persian painting shows a view of life in a desert camp.

Fighting took the form of raids on other tribes' flocks. The object was partly to gain booty. But just as important was the glory that could be won by showing bravery and daring. The bedouin celebrated their raids in poems, which were memorized and passed from one generation to another.

Scattered throughout the desert were oases, places with water. Here some Arabs settled and grew crops, which they traded with the bedouin for wool.

Trade with other countries was also important. Arabia's caravan routes linked the Mediterranean with India and the Far East. Huge camel trains travelled across the deserts, carrying perfumes from southern Arabia, spices, silk and precious metals from the East, and ivory from Africa. At the crossroads of the trade routes was the town of Mecca, home of the Quraish tribe. The Quraish were merchants and they controlled much of the caravan trade.

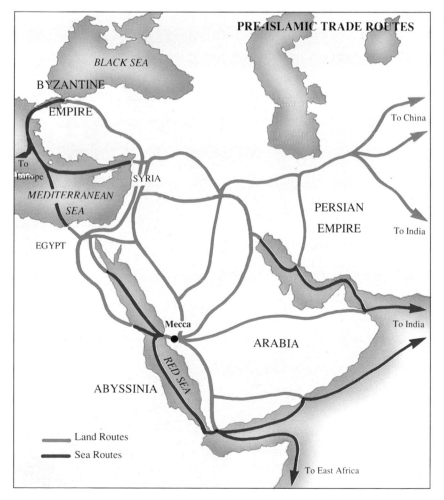

Mecca owed its wealth and importance to its position on the trade routes.

Left *Even today, some Arabs still have a traditional nomadic lifestyle in the desert regions of North Africa and the Middle East.*

Right *A Turkish tile showing the Kaaba, a cube-shaped temple covered in black cloth, at the centre of a plan of the great mosque of Mecca. The Kaaba was a place for pilgrimages long before Islam.*

Mecca was also an important religious centre. The Arabs worshipped many gods and spirits, which they believed lived in rocks, trees and wells. At Mecca, there was a cube-shaped temple called the Kaaba. Here various gods were worshipped, together with a supreme god called Allah. The Kaaba also contained a sacred black stone, probably a meteorite. Each year, people from all over Arabia would travel to Mecca, on a pilgrimage to the Kaaba. The Quraish held big fairs for the pilgrims.

By the seventh century however, some Arabs had become dissatisfied with their old religion. Through trade they came into contact with Christians who lived in Syria, Egypt and Abyssinia. They were also influenced by Jewish tribes living in the oasis settlements. Both the Christians and the Jews claimed that there was only one god; they looked down on the Arab religion as superstitious idol worship. Some Arabs converted to these religions. Other Arabs, called *hanifs*, also came to believe in a single god, though they adopted neither Judaism nor Christianity.

Muhammad

Muhammad, the founder of Islam, was born in Mecca around AD 570. He belonged to one of the poorer families of the Quraish tribe. As a young man he was employed by a wealthy widow called Khadija, whose goods he took to Syria in the camel train. Khadija was so impressed by Muhammad's personality and skill in business that she asked him to marry her. This marriage gave Muhammad financial security.

According to one tradition, Muhammad forbade art showing people or animals. As a result, Muslim artists concentrated on rich patterns and decorative writing. The Alhambra palace at Granada in Spain is covered with lines of poetry and phrases from the Koran such as, 'There is no conqueror but Allah'.

In this Persian painting, Muhammad and his family are visited by holy men and an angel. Persian artists often ignored the ban on representations of people; but as a sign of respect, they usually veiled Muhammad's face.

After his marriage, Muhammad began to visit the mountains outside Mecca in order to be alone and think. It was here, around 610, that he had an experience that changed his life; he believed he had received a message from God. According to Muslim tradition, the Angel Gabriel appeared to him and said: 'Recite!' At first, Muhammad did not know what to make of this experience. But after a while, he felt he was receiving more messages, including the command to preach the messages publicly.

Muhammad preached that there was only one god, Allah; that it was everyone's duty to submit to the will of Allah; that after death, believers would be rewarded in Paradise while unbelievers would burn in Hell; and that all believers were equal before Allah.

This message annoyed the wealthy merchants of Mecca. His attack on their gods threatened the pilgrimage trade to the Kaaba. His claim that the poor were as good as the rich was also an attack on their social status. But Muhammad began to make converts, particularly among the young and the poor.

Muhammad met with such hostility that he decided to leave Mecca. In 622, he moved with his followers to the town of Yathrib, later known as Medina (which means 'the city' in Arabic). Muhammad was no longer simply a religious preacher; he became the leader of the first Muslim community, with political and military power. His messages also changed in character; they were now concerned with practical rules for everyday living. The migration, or *hijra*, to Medina marks the first year of the Muslim calendar.

Because the Meccans had rejected his preaching, Muhammad decided that they would have to be convinced by force. He began to organize raids on their camel trains. He was joined by several bedouin tribes, attracted by the prospect of booty and the promise of Paradise if they were killed in battle. The Meccans fought back, but the number of converts to Islam continued to grow. In 630, Muhammad marched on Mecca with 10,000 men. He captured the town and destroyed the images of the gods in the Kaaba. This shrine, which he claimed had been built by the Jewish prophet Abraham, now became Islam's holiest place.

Muhammad was both a military and a religious leader. In this, another Persian illustration, he directs the siege of a town. Unusually, Muhammad's face is shown. Although this picture was drawn by an Islamic artist, some Muslims would feel that it shows a lack of respect for the Prophet.

The Muslim victory convinced many Arabs that their old gods were powerless. The wealthy Meccans converted to Islam and they were followed by more and more Arab tribes. By the time of Muhammad's death in 632, the whole of western Arabia was Muslim.

Muslims believe that Muhammad regularly received messages from God. These messages were memorized or written down by his followers. After Muhammad's death, they were made into a book called the Koran (which means 'recitation' in Arabic). It is very different to the Jewish and Christian holy books. The Bible talks about God but, to a Muslim, the Koran is the speech of God himself. In this extract, God is telling the Arab people that he has sent them a messenger (Muhammad) just as he has previously sent messengers to other races:

We have sent forth to you a messenger of your own who will recite to you Our revelations and purify you of sin, who will instruct you in the Book and in wisdom and teach you that of which you had no knowledge. Remember Me then, and I will remember you.

(The Koran, Sura [Chapter] Two)

Muslims believe that the Koran is Allah's final message to the world, correcting all previous holy books. Since every word is thought to have been actually spoken by Allah himself, Muslim calligraphers took great care to produce beautiful copies of the holy book.

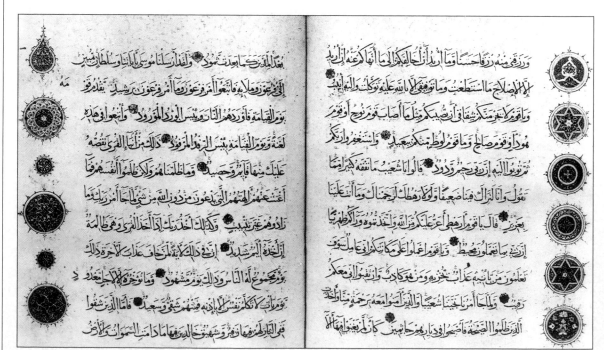

The Arab Conquests

In the century after Muhammad's death, the Arab armies burst out of the desert and conquered an empire stretching from India to Spain. This was the largest empire the world had seen.

The Arab conquerors were driven by religious enthusiasm. Muhammad had told them that it was a Muslim's duty to fight a jihad, or holy war, against unbelievers. Since God was on their side, victory was certain; anyone killed fighting a holy war would be rewarded in Paradise.

To the bedouin tribesmen, this was a very powerful idea. Fighting had always been a part of their lives, but previously they had fought each other. Now they were united under the banner of Islam. The bedouin were also attracted by the wealth of the lands they invaded. They soon realized that wars against foreigners were much more profitable than their old tribal conflicts.

During the first two centuries after Muhammad's death, Islam spread rapidly throughout North Africa and the Middle East.

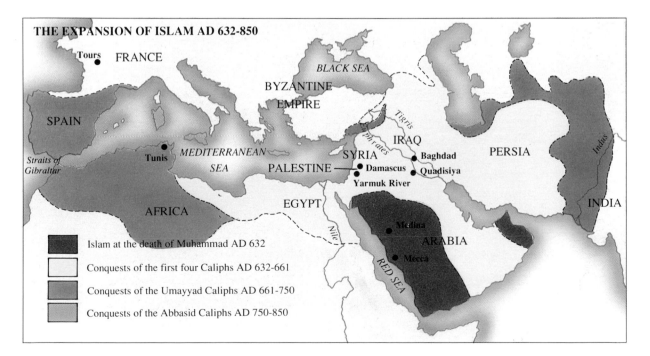

THE EXPANSION OF ISLAM AD 632-850

Islam at the death of Muhammad AD 632

Conquests of the first four Caliphs AD 632-661

Conquests of the Umayyad Caliphs AD 661-750

Conquests of the Abbasid Caliphs AD 750-850

The purpose of holy war was to spread the power of Islam. However, the Arabs did not believe in forcing everyone to become a Muslim. People could still practise Judaism, Christianity or Zoroastrianism (the religion of Persia). But they had to accept Islamic rule and pay a special tax to their conquerors. To avoid paying this tax, many people converted to Islam.

The Arabs chose just the right moment to begin their conquests. North of Arabia lay the great empires of Persia and Byzantium. These empires were exhausted after a war against each other that had lasted twenty-six years (602–628). To pay for this war, they had imposed higher and higher taxes on the people they ruled. The Persian and Byzantine rulers were so hated that the Arab armies were often welcomed as liberators.

The people of Syria and Egypt had an extra reason to hate their Byzantine rulers. They were Christian, but they followed different forms of Christianity to the Byzantines. The

This eleventh-century Greek chronicle shows a skirmish between Arab soldiers, who carry round shields, and Byzantines, who flee, deserting their general. Despite regular attempts, the Arabs were unable to conquer the whole of the Byzantine Empire.

Byzantines had tried to stamp out all kinds of Christianity other than their own. Syrian and Egyptian Christians found that the Arabs were much more tolerant than their Byzantine rulers.

Another reason for the Arabs' success was their way of fighting. The Persian and Byzantine armies were slow moving; they relied on calvalrymen who wore heavy coats of armour. In contrast, the lightly-armoured Arabs relied on speed and surprise. They were used to fighting in the desert conditions and could travel quickly across great distances with very few supplies.

In 636, the Arabs destroyed the Byzantine army at the Yarmuk river in Syria. In the same year, they also defeated the Persians at Qadisiya in Iraq. After conquering Syria and Palestine, they advanced west into Egypt and North Africa. Meanwhile, other Arab armies were moving east, over-running the Persian empire. By 711, they had even reached Sind in north-west India.

After the conquest of North Africa, its native people, called Berbers, became dedicated Muslims. It was a Berber

Above *A Christian tombstone from Egypt, showing a praying woman. The Christians of Egypt belonged to the Coptic Church, which was very different from the Orthodox Church of the Byzantines. Many Copts welcomed Arab rule.*

Left *To show that they were fighting for Allah, Muslim armies carried banners inscribed with phrases from the Koran. This is a thirteenth-century Spanish illustration. The first Muslim armies were much less heavily armed.*

army, led by Arab generals, that took the holy war into Europe. In 711, the Berbers crossed the Straits of Gibraltar and invaded Spain. Within ten years they had conquered Spain and crossed into France. Their advance was not halted until 732, when they were defeated by a French army near the city of Tours.

According to the Koran, Muslims had a duty to fight a jihad, or holy war, against unbelievers:

Let those who would exchange the life of this world for the hereafter fight for the cause of Allah; whether they die or conquer, We shall richly reward them.

(The Koran, Sura [Chapter] Four)

It was the custom for Arabs to send letters to a country they intended to invade. Here is one such letter, written in 633 by a famous general called Khalid, nicknamed 'the Sword of Islam':

In the name of God, the Merciful and the Compassionate.

From Khalid ibn al-Walid to the border chiefs of Persia.
Become Muslim and be saved. If not, accept protection from us and pay the tax.
If not, I shall come against you with men who love death as you love to drink wine.

(Quoted by the historian al-Tabari [838-923], *Annals*)

Why did Khalid say that his men loved death?

A coin of the Umayyad caliph, Abd al-Malik. He holds the 'Sword of Islam', a symbol of his authority which he carried when he led the public prayers in the mosque.

The Islamic World

By 750, the great period of Arab conquest was over. However, Islam continued to spread, because of trade and missionary activity. Arab merchants sailed the Indian Ocean in dhows, boats built of teak or coconut planks, rigged with a lateen, or triangular, sail. They founded trading settlements on the coasts of East Africa, India, Indonesia and China. They sold luxury goods from Arabia – decorative metalwork, painted pottery and carpets. In Africa, they traded these goods for slaves, ivory and gold. India and Indonesia provided spices, and China was a source of silk, porcelain, paper and ink.

Arab merchants also travelled by land, across the Sahara desert to the kingdoms of West Africa. Another trade route was the Volga river, which linked the Arabs with the Vikings who lived around the Baltic. Viking merchants sold furs, amber and armour to the Arabs.

The Arab traders practised and preached their religion. They were followed by Muslim teachers and missionaries. As a result, many people converted to Islam. The missionaries had the greatest success in Africa, Central Asia and Indonesia. In 1010, the ruler of Gao in West Africa became Muslim. Seventy-seven years later, a Muslim university was founded nearby, at Timbuctu. Its library was famous, attracting scholars from all over the Muslim world.

The people of Central Asia were called Turks. Like the bedouin, they were nomads who lived by herding cattle and by warfare. In the tenth century, many of the Turkish tribes were converted by missionaries. Later, it was Turkish armies that carried Islam deep into India, though traders and missionaries also played a part. Between the eleventh and fourteenth centuries, waves of Turkish invaders conquered much of the Indian continent. Traders and missionaries from India then took Islam to Indonesia and the Philippines, where many people were converted between the thirteenth and sixteenth centuries.

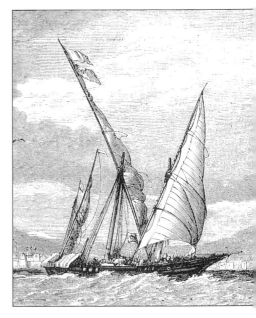

This nineteenth-century British engraving shows a dhow, an Arab trading ship. Dhows still sail the Indian Ocean.

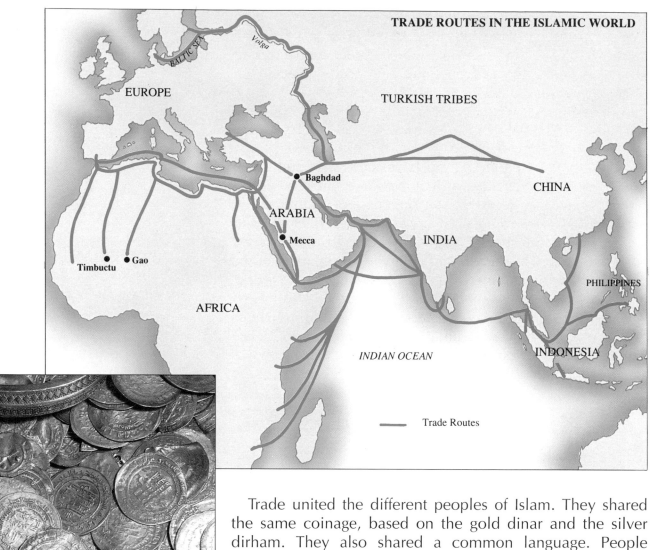

EUROPE

TURKISH TRIBES

BALTIC SEA

Volga

Baghdad

CHINA

ARABIA

Mecca

INDIA

Gao

Timbuctu

PHILIPPINES

AFRICA

INDONESIA

INDIAN OCEAN

—— Trade Routes

Trade, as much as warfare, encouraged the spread of Islam. Discoveries of Arab coins show us the extent of this trade. This hoard was found in a tenth-century Viking grave in Sweden.

Trade united the different peoples of Islam. They shared the same coinage, based on the gold dinar and the silver dirham. They also shared a common language. People throughout Islam learned Arabic. It was the language of government. More important, it was the language of the Koran. Muslims believed that God had chosen to give his message in Arabic. It would be wrong to translate the Koran into another language.

The Koran contained many instructions for everyday living. Alcohol, gambling and certain foods, such as pork, were forbidden. There were also rules for the conduct of family life and the treatment of slaves. These instructions formed the basis for a system of holy laws called the sharia. The sharia was also based on decisions and actions which were supposed to have been made by Muhammad during his lifetime. Through the Koran and the sharia, many different peoples came to share a similar way of life.

Every Muslim was expected to perform five acts, which are known as the 'Five Pillars of Islam'. The first was the declaration made by every Muslim in order to become a Muslim: 'There is no god but Allah and Muhammad is the messenger of Allah'.

Prayer, the second pillar, was performed by all Muslims five times a day – at sunrise, midday, late afternoon, sunset and evening. The worshipper had to be in a state of purity, achieved by washing the hands, lower arms, feet and head. If water was not available, sand or even dust could be used.

Muslims always faced in the direction of Mecca when they prayed. They could pray anywhere, in the street or at home. In addition, special places for prayer called mosques were built. Every mosque had a courtyard and a minaret, or tower. When it was time to pray, a man called a muezzin would climb the minaret and call the faithful: 'Come to prayer! Come to security!' Inside the mosque, there would be a covered prayer hall with a mihrab, a niche in the wall showing the direction of Mecca. Mosques might also serve as law courts, schools and public meeting places.

A Muslim at prayer in the mosque at Samarkand in the USSR. He faces a niche in the wall showing the direction of Mecca.

Above Left *An engraving of the Great Mosque of Delhi in India, built in the 1640s. All mosques share certain features, such as the minarets, or towers; but their architectural style varies from one country to another. These bulb-shaped domes are typical of Indian architecture.*

Above Right *This man, photographed in the bazaar of Isfahan in Persia, wears a black band to show that he has been on the pilgrimage to Mecca. At the end of each annual pilgrimage, the kiswah, the black cloth covering the Kaaba, is cut into small pieces which are distributed to the pilgrims.*

The third pillar was the poor tax. Believers were expected to give a small part of their earnings in tax to be distributed to the poor. By doing so, they were thought to purify the rest of their money.

Fasting, the fourth pillar, took place during Ramadan, the ninth month in the Muslim year. From dawn to dusk in Ramadan, Muslims were expected to give up food and drink. Travellers and sick people were allowed to postpone the fast until a later date.

The last pillar was the hajj, or pilgrimage, to Mecca and Medina. Once in a lifetime, every Muslim was supposed to travel to the holy cities of Islam. This pilgrimage took place once a year, two months after Ramadan. It brought together thousands of Muslims, rich and poor, from many different races. They would dress alike to show that they were all equal before God. Together, they would perform certain ceremonies, such as walking around the Kaaba seven times. The pilgrimage brought together scholars, who could exchange ideas, and merchants, who could discuss trade. Through the pilgrimage, Muslims learned about distant lands. It gave them the feeling that they belonged to a single, vast community.

In some respects, Islam improved the position of women. Previously, Arab men could marry as many wives as they wanted and they were free to mistreat them. Muhammad limited the number of wives a man could have to four, and he could only have this many if he could treat them equally and fairly. Women's rights to inherit and own property were also improved. However, the Arab world was still very much controlled by men:

Men have authority over women because Allah has made the one superior to the other, and because they spend their wealth to maintain them. Good women are obedient. As for those from whom you fear disobedience, warn them and send them to beds apart and beat them. Then if they obey you, take no further action against them.
(The Koran, Sura [Chapter] Four)

Although the Koran states that women are inferior to men, the position of women has varied in different historical periods and from one Islamic country to another. Some Muslim women are expected to wear veils and live secluded lives, but these Persian women, in a sixteenth-century painting, have much greater freedom.

The Caliphate

In Muhammad's lifetime, Arabs did not mint their own coins at all. Then the first caliphs copied the coins of the lands they ruled. The Umayyad silver dirham on the left is a copy of a Persian coin; the strange winged headgear was worn by Persian kings. The coin on the right is an Abbasid silver dirham – the horse and rider were also copied from earlier models. Such coins were eventually replaced with coins bearing only inscriptions from the Koran.

Muhammad died without naming a successor, or explaining how one could be chosen. To solve this problem, the most important Muslims elected a caliph, which means 'successor' and 'deputy'. The caliph was both a religious and a political leader and was also known as the Commander of the Faithful. The first four caliphs were devout Muslims who had been close companions of Muhammad. They were later known as the 'rightly-guided' caliphs.

The fourth caliph, Ali, who was Muhammad's son-in-law and cousin, died in 661. A single family, the Umayyads, then took over the caliphate. The Umayyads were one of the wealthy ruling families of Mecca, and they had opposed Muhammad during his lifetime. They were more like kings than religious leaders. From 661 to 750, the Umayyad caliphs ruled the Empire from their capital city, Damascus.

Some Muslims believed that the Umayyads had no right to rule. They said that only a member of Muhammad's family could be caliph and so they recognized only Ali, the fourth caliph. These people were known as the shiites (pronounced 'sheeites') because they belonged to the *shia* or 'party' of Ali. After Ali's death in 661, the shiites transferred their loyalty to his sons and descendants.

Muhammad with his closest companions, Abu Bekr, Umar, Uthman and Ali. These men would later be the first four caliphs of Islam, the so-called 'rightly-guided' caliphs.

Ali's eldest son, Hasan, was either bribed or forced by the Umayyads to give up his claim to the caliphate – shiite historians favour the second explanation. But Ali's second son, Hosein, rebelled against the Umayyads. In 680, he set out from Medina to Iraq, where he expected to be proclaimed as caliph. He was accompanied by his family and less than two hundred supporters. At Kerbela in Iraq, they were met by a much larger Umayyad army. Hosein and all of his followers were massacred.

The Umayyad dynasty was founded by a man called Muawiya, who became caliph in 661. According to a shiite historian, al-Isfahani (897–967), Hasan, the grandson of Muhammad, wrote to Muawiya:

You, Oh Muawiya, are trying to take an authority you do not deserve. You do not possess any known merit in religion. On the contrary, you are the son of the greatest enemy of the Prophet. So give up your persistence in falsehood, for you are certainly aware that I am far more entitled to the caliphate than you in the eyes of God and all worthy people.

Muawiya replied:

Had I believed that you could protect the community better than I, and that you were stronger in safeguarding the properties of Muslims and outwitting the enemy than I, then I would have done what you have asked me. But I am more experienced, better in policies and older than you.
(Quoted by al-Isfahani, *Lives of Martyrs*)

What qualities did each man believe that a caliph should possess?

Below *This is a carving of Darius I, the great king who ruled the Persian Empire more than a thousand years before the time of Muhammad. Proud of their ancient civilization, many Persians resented Arab rule.*

To the shiites, Hosein – Muhammad's grandson – was now a glorious martyr. Even today, the anniversary of Hosein's death is a day of mourning for shiite Muslims, and Kerbela is a shiite holy city.

The Kerbela massacre made shiism a powerful religious movement. The shiites said that the Umayyads had betrayed Islam; they had brought tyranny instead of justice to the world. Nevertheless, God would one day send a true Imam, or leader. This Imam would be a descendant of Ali and would bring peace and justice. He was later known as the Mahdi, the 'rightly-guided one'. Over the years, many people came forward claiming to be the awaited Mahdi.

Shiism spread among the poor and discontented. It drew most support from Muslims who were not Arabs, especially Persians. Muhammad had said that all Muslims were equal, regardless of race. But the Umayyads treated foreigners as if they were inferior to Arabs, taxing them more heavily. As the Persians had an older civilization than the Arabs and were often better educated, they bitterly resented such treatment by the Umayyads.

Persia was the birthplace of the rebellion that eventually overthrew the Umayyads. The rebel leaders were called the Abbasids because they were descended from Muhammad's uncle, Abbas. They circulated poems attacking the Umayyads and extracts from the Koran denouncing evil government.

Such writings are called propaganda. The Abbasid propaganda said that the Umayyads were not true caliphs: they were worldly people who were unfit to rule. The only hope lay in giving supreme power to the family of Muhammad. Many shiites took part in this revolutionary movement, believing that the caliphate would go to Ali's family. But in fact the Abbasids used the shiites to get power for themselves.

In 747, the Abbasids rose in open rebellion. Their army wore black clothes and carried black banners, a colour associated with the Abbasid family. They defeated the Umayyads in Persia, and then moved west. Within three years, the Umayyads had been overthrown.

Now the rebel leader, Abu Abbas, became caliph. He called himself al-Saffah, the shedder of blood, and it was a name he lived up to. During his reign (750–4) almost all the members of the Umayyad family were killed. On one occasion, seventy-two Umayyads were invited to a banquet, supposedly as a peace gesture. Halfway through the meal, armed soldiers entered the hall and slaughtered them.

Only one Umayyad escaped, a young man called Abd al-Rahman. He fled to Spain, where he was welcomed as Amir, or ruler. His descendants ruled most of Spain for three hundred years.

The shiites were also treated brutally. Far from helping their cause, the Abbasids had members of the family of Ali imprisoned. Like the Umayyads, once in power the Abbasids identified themselves with the majority of Muslims, or sunnis. Shiism now began to provide a focus for opposition to the Abbasid caliphate.

Although the Umayyad caliphs were overthrown in 750, the family continued to rule in Spain for centuries. This ivory casket, made in the tenth century, comes from Cordoba, the Umayyad capital. At this time, Cordoba was the largest and wealthiest city in Europe.

The Abbasid Caliphs of Baghdad

Under the Umayyads, all important posts had been held by Arabs. Other races had been treated as inferior. This situation changed when the Abbasid caliphs seized power. Although they were themselves Arabs, the Abbasids owed their success to support from Persian Muslims. As a result, they allowed Persians and other non-Arabs to reach high positions. The Islamic Empire became international in character.

In 762, the caliph, al-Mansur, founded a new capital city, Baghdad in Iraq. It was built where two great rivers, the Tigris and the Euphrates, came closest together. It was an important crossroads for trade.

Baghdad was built as a round city, about three kilometres across, surrounded by two strong walls. At its very centre stood the palace of the caliph. Only the caliph, his soldiers and officials lived inside the round city. Ordinary people lived in houses outside the walls, where a vast commercial area grew. By 814, Baghdad was the world's largest city.

This thirteenth-century illustration gives us an idea of ordinary life in an Islamic city. The picture shows a school, with two teachers arguing on the left. On the right, one student operates a fan while the other students listen.

Ibn Wadih al-Yaqubi, a ninth-century historian, wrote a description of Baghdad:

I begin with Iraq because it is the centre of the world, and I mention Baghdad first because it is the centre of Iraq, the greatest city, which has no equal in the world in size, wealth, abundance of water or health of climate, and because it is inhabited by all kinds of people. To it they come from all countries, far and near. Goods and foodstuffs come to it by land and by water, so that every kind of merchandise is available, from Muslim and from non-Muslim lands. Goods are brought from India, China, the lands of the Turks, the Ethiopians and others to such an extent that the products of the countries are more plentiful in Baghdad than in the countries from which they come. It is as if all the good things of the earth are sent there.

(Ibn Wadih al-Yaqubi, *Universal History*)

Why do you think this historian thought that Iraq was the centre of the world? Why was Baghdad described as the most important city of all?

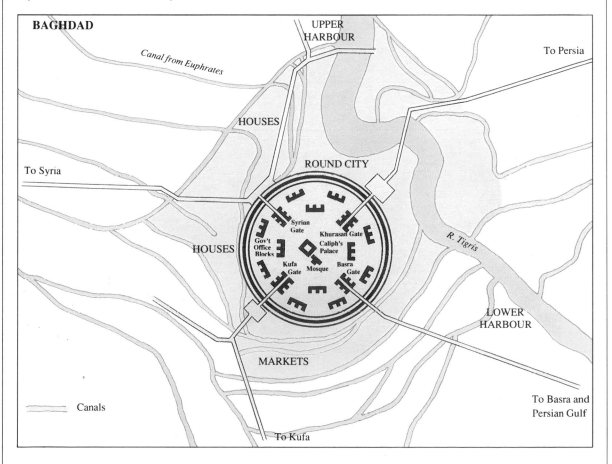

BAGHDAD
UPPER HARBOUR
To Persia
Canal from Euphrates
HOUSES
ROUND CITY
To Syria
Syrian Gate
Khurasan Gate
Gov't Office Blocks
Caliph's Palace
HOUSES
Kufa Gate
Mosque
Basra Gate
R. Tigris
LOWER HARBOUR
MARKETS
Canals
To Kufa
To Basra and Persian Gulf

Baghdad, the Abbasid capital, with the caliph's palace at its centre. The city grew rapidly until it covered a large area, around 100 square kilometres in size.

Living in very dry countries, Muslims became expert at building irrigation machines, such as these water wheels on the river Orontes in Syria. Driven by the force of the river, the wheels scooped up the water and emptied it into channels; it would then flow out to water the fields.

The Umayyads had ruled like traditional Arab chieftains, mixing freely with their subjects. In contrast, the Abbasids copied the style of Persian kings, rulers who had absolute power and were treated almost as gods. The Abbasid caliph sat on a raised throne, hidden behind a curtain. People who were ushered into his presence were expected to kiss the floor at his feet. Behind the throne stood an executioner with a drawn sword, ready to behead anyone who displeased the caliph.

The Abbasids stressed their religious authority. They said they were 'the Shadow of God on Earth' and they adopted religious names, such as al-Mansur, which means 'the one helped to victory [by God]'. Another caliph was al-Rashid, 'the rightly-guided one'.

While the caliph was a remote figure, day-to-day government was handled by the vizier, a word originally meaning 'helper'. The vizier was like a combination of prime minister and chief civil servant. He could become immensely rich and powerful.

Unlike the Umayyads, the Abbasids did not conquer vast new lands for Islam. They were more interested in the benefits of peace – the growth of industry and trade. There were advances in technology. Farming was improved by the use of machines for irrigation (the supply of water to dry areas) and by the draining of swamps.

Muslims also learned how to make paper. They were taught by Chinese paper-makers, captured in battle in 751. Previously people had written on papyrus leaves. The use of paper made books cheaper and also encouraged the spread of learning.

Another new development was banking, including the use of cheques (a word which comes from the Arabic *sakk*). A cheque from a bank in Baghdad could be cashed as far away as a bank in Morocco.

The most famous Abbasid caliph was Harun al-Rashid, who ruled from 786 to 809. This was the high point of Abbasid power. The caliph sent ambassadors to the courts of the French king, Charlemagne, and the emperor of China. Harun al-Rashid is best known today as a fictional character in the *Arabian Nights*, a collection of folk tales from India, Persia, Arabia and Egypt. This book was itself a product of the trade links created by Islam.

After al-Rashid, the caliphs came to rely on Turkish slaves as their soldiers and bodyguards. As their influence grew, these Turks realized that whoever controlled the caliph could rule in his name. The Abbasids became helpless puppets, appointed and deposed at the will of their guards. Between 847 and 974, six caliphs were murdered and three others were imprisoned and blinded.

Meanwhile the Abbasids began to lose control of the provinces. Sometimes a local governor became so powerful that he could not be replaced. He handed on his authority to his son, thus founding an independent dynasty.

Most of these rulers still accepted in theory at least the Abbasid caliph as the head of Islam. However, in 909 a man called Ubayd Allah seized power in North Africa. He said that he was the Mahdi, the true ruler of Islam awaited by shiite Muslims. Members of his family were called the Fatimids, because they claimed to be descended from Muhammad's daughter, Fatima. They built their own capital city, Cairo, in Egypt. By 978, the Fatimid army had also conquered most of Syria.

An ivory carving of a musician from Fatimid Egypt. He plays a lute or 'ud, the most popular of Islamic instruments. Music was played in the caliph's court but also for ordinary people, at weddings and festivals.

The minaret of a mosque built by the Seljuks. They founded a powerful dynasty based in central and eastern Turkey.

For a while, it looked as if the Abbasids would be overthrown. But they were rescued by a new Turkish tribe, led by a family called the Seljuks. The Seljuks were fierce fighters who were dedicated to the holy war. They were also Sunni Muslims who hated the shiite Fatimids. In 1055, the caliph gave the Seljuk leader the title of sultan, which means 'power' or 'authority'. From now on, all political and military power would be held by the Seljuk sultan. The caliph would only have religious authority. In 1071, the Seljuks defeated the Byzantines, and conquered much of eastern Turkey. Seven years later, they drove the Fatimids out of Syria and created a Seljuk Empire. It was ruled by the sultan in the name of the Abbasid caliph of Baghdad.

The Crusades

Between 1096 and 1291, the Christian peoples of Europe made a series of military expeditions to the Middle East. Their aim was to capture Jerusalem, the city where Christ died and was buried. These expeditions were called Crusades from the Latin word *crux* or cross. The wars were fought in the name of the Christian religion.

For Muslims, the holiest place in Jerusalem was the Dome of the Rock, built where Muhammad was believed to have climbed into heaven up a ladder of light. The Crusaders converted this Muslim shrine into a Christian church.

The French King Philip II defeats the Muslim army during the Third Crusade. Despite this heroic image, Philip spent most of his time in the Holy Land sick in his tent, or quarrelling with the English king, Richard.

Jerusalem was a holy city for Muslims as well as for Jews and Christians. Muslims honoured Jesus (called *Isa* in Arabic) and the Jewish prophets as messengers of God, like Muhammad. There was also a tradition that Muhammad had visited Jerusalem in a vision. From Jerusalem, he was believed to have been taken up into heaven.

For centuries, even though the city had been in Muslim hands, Christian pilgrims had been free to visit the tomb of Christ. However, in the eleventh century Palestine was overrun by the Seljuk Turks. There was a fear that the Turks would make it much harder for Christian pilgrims to travel to Jerusalem.

In this period, the knights of Europe lived by constant warfare, usually against each other. Pope Urban II decided that they would be better occupied fighting Muslims than fellow Christians. In 1095, he called for a holy war to rescue Christ's tomb from the unbelievers. He said that people

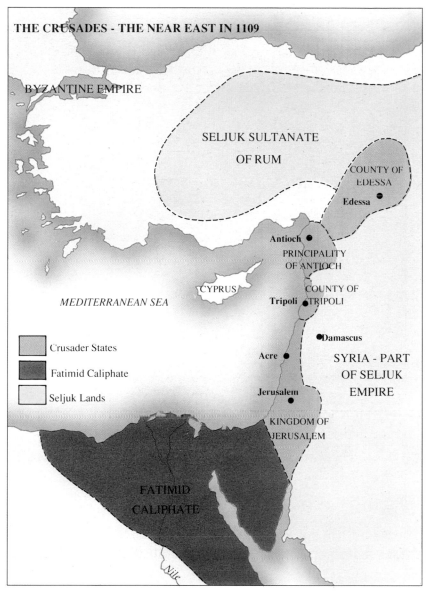

THE CRUSADES - THE NEAR EAST IN 1109

BYZANTINE EMPIRE

SELJUK SULTANATE
OF RUM

COUNTY OF
EDESSA

Edessa

Antioch
PRINCIPALITY
OF ANTIOCH

CYPRUS

COUNTY OF
TRIPOLI

MEDITERRANEAN SEA

Tripoli

Damascus

Acre

SYRIA - PART
OF SELJUK
EMPIRE

Jerusalem

Crusader States

Fatimid Caliphate

Seljuk Lands

KINGDOM OF
JERUSALEM

FATIMID
CALIPHATE

Nile

The knights of the First Crusade created four Christian states in the Middle East. These were safe only as long as Muslim rulers were divided amongst themselves.

who fought in the holy war would be fighting for God, and would earn forgiveness for their sins. The Crusaders were also encouraged by the promise of bringing home wealth and booty from the Holy Land.

The Crusade was as attractive to the knights as Muhammad's holy war had been to the Arab tribesmen. A wave of religious enthusiasm swept across Europe. A huge army assembled, including Normans, Italians, Germans, English and Franks, or Frenchmen. To the Muslims, they were *all* called Franks. Similarly, the Crusaders called all Muslims either Turks or Saracens.

The Crusaders had no idea of the distances they would have to travel or of the sort of place that they were going to. Thousands of people died of heat and thirst on the journey. Nevertheless, in June 1099, they reached the holy city. After a month's siege, Jerusalem was captured. The Crusaders ran through the streets, massacring every man, woman and child they could find. Jews as well as Muslims were killed, for they were also thought to be the enemies of God.

The Crusaders created four Christian states in the East – Jerusalem, Antioch, Tripoli and Edessa. In Europe, these were known as Outremer, the land beyond the sea. Outremer had to fight for its survival. In 1144, the Turks recaptured Edessa. A Second Crusade was organized, but failed to achieve anything.

The First Crusade had succeeded because the Muslims were divided. The Seljuks, sunni Muslims, had been fighting the shiite Fatimids. The Seljuks were also divided among

The great crusading castle of Krak des Chevaliers in northern Syria. A Christian stronghold for 161 years, it was finally captured by the Muslims in 1271.

Usama ibn Munquidh (1095–1188) was a Syrian who came into contact with many Franks, or Europeans. His memoirs show us how Crusaders appeared to Muslims:

The Franks are animals, having only the virtues of courage and fighting, but nothing else, just as animals have only the virtues of strength and carrying loads. There are some Franks who have settled in our land and taken to living like Muslims. These are better than those who have just arrived from their homelands, but they are the exception.
(Usama ibn Munquidh, *Memoirs*)

Here is another description of the Franks, by the writer, al-Qazwini:

Their soldiers are of mighty courage and in the hour of combat do not even think of flight, rather preferring death. But you shall see none more filthy than they. They do not wash more than twice a year. They shave their beards, and after shaving they sprout only a revolting stubble.
(Al-Qazwini, *Historical Geography*)

Did these writers find anything to admire about the Franks?

Most pictures of crusading battles were painted by European monks who had never seen a Muslim soldier. Despite their dark faces and Arab headgear, these Muslims are armed like European knights.

themselves. Throughout their lands there were many rival rulers. These had been so busy fighting each other that they had not noticed the threat from the Crusaders until it was too late. The caliph and the rulers of Iraq and Persia left the local rulers to deal with the Crusaders on their own.

In the 1180s Syria and Palestine were reunited under a strong leader. His name was Salah-al-Din or, as he was known to the Crusaders, Saladin. He was a sunni, loyal to the Abbasid caliph in Baghdad. In 1171, Saladin overthrew the rival Fatimid caliphate of Cairo. His rule then spread from Egypt to Syria and northern Iraq. Outremer was now threatened by a united Muslim empire called the Ayyubid Sultanate, after Saladin's father, Ayyub.

Saladin was dedicated to the jihad, the Muslim holy war, and he was determined to recapture Jerusalem. In 1187, his army defeated the Christians at Hattin near the Sea of Galilee. One by one, the kingdoms of Outremer surrendered. Soon, the holy city itself was captured. But unlike the previous conquerors, the Muslims did not kill a single person after their victory.

A Third Crusade followed, led by Richard the Lionheart of England and Philip of France. This crusade was able to conquer only a narrow coastal strip. Year by year, this territory grew smaller. In 1291, the city of Acre, the last outpost of Outremer, fell to the Muslims.

From the Muslim point of view, the Franks were ignorant savages. The Crusades were a series of barbarian invasions: destructive, but of little long-term importance. In contrast, the Europeans were changed by their contact with Muslims. They developed a taste for sugar, spices, rice, oranges and melons. The wealthier began to dress in silk and cotton instead of furs and wool. They learned to build magnificent stone castles. They were also introduced to Arab science and medicine, superior to anything in Europe.

Muslim silks were highly prized in Europe. This cloth, embroidered with lions and palm trees, was made in Bukhara, Central Asia, between the eighth and ninth century. In the eleventh century, it was taken to France where it was used to wrap the bones of Saint Amon.

The Ottoman Empire

In the thirteenth century the Byzantine Empire was falling apart and the Seljuk Empire had ceased to exist. Constantinople, the Byzantine capital, had been sacked by Crusaders in 1204 and had never really recovered. Muslim countries had also been attacked, by a fierce race from central Asia called the Mongols. In 1258, the Mongols captured Baghdad and killed thousands of its inhabitants, including the caliph. This disaster shocked the Muslim world.

The collapse of these empires allowed a new Turkish family to rise to power. They were called the Ottomans, after their founder, Osman. From 1281 to 1324, Osman was ruler of a tiny state in Turkey, close to the Byzantine border. He saw himself as a Ghazi, a warrior in the holy war. Because his state was so close to Byzantine lands, Osman attracted many other Turkish Ghazis, warriors who saw the opportunity of land and plunder. These Turks fought on horseback and were called *sipahis*. They gave their military services to the Ottomans in exchange for grants of land and money.

Osman's son, Orkhan, took the title of sultan. During his reign (1324–62), the Ottomans crossed into Europe and began their conquest of the Balkans. By 1400, they had conquered Serbia, Bulgaria and most of the Byzantine Empire.

The Ottomans developed a remarkable method for running their empire. It relied on slavery. Today, we think of slavery as hard labour and assume that slaves are the lowest level of society. But Ottoman slavery was quite different.

Instead of taking money taxes from the peasants of the Balkans, the Ottomans began to take their boy children, aged between six and fifteen. These Christian boys would then be educated and brought up as Muslims. Some would join an infantry force called the janizaries (from *yeni cheri* Turkish for 'new troops'). Others were trained for careers in government. The ablest might rise to the highest posts in the Empire. As a result, the people who ruled the Ottoman Empire were usually not even Turks by birth, but Europeans.

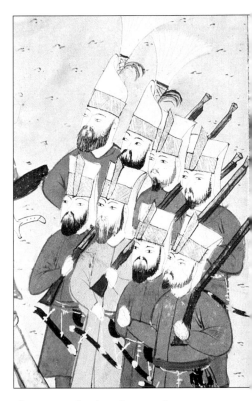

Ottoman janizaries or slave infantrymen. Each is armed with a musket and a long curved knife called a yataghan. The janizaries were the most feared soldiers in the sultan's army.

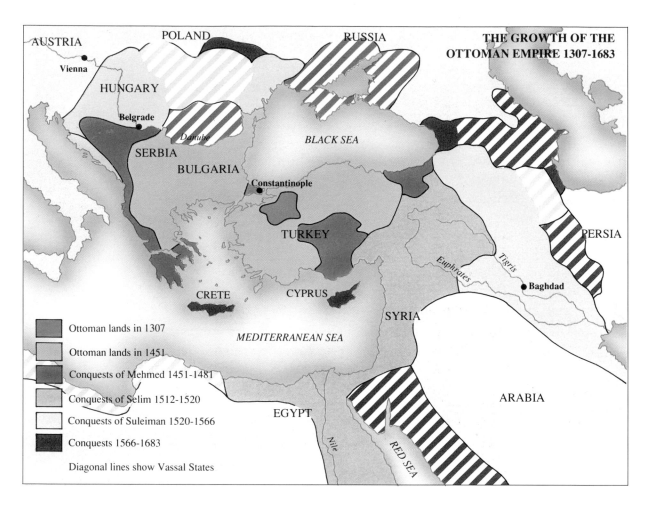

Like the Arabs before them, the Ottoman Turks conquered a vast empire for Islam.

For the boys it must have been a strange experience, taken away from their homes by foreigners. But they were offered opportunities which they would never have had in their peasant villages. The advantage for the sultan was that these slaves were more likely to be loyal than free Turks, or even members of his own family. The janizaries, more reliable than the *sipahis*, became the best soldiers in the sultan's army.

Unlike most European governments, the Ottomans allowed people to practise different religions. Some of the lands they conquered had been ruled by Roman Catholics who persecuted different types of Christianity. In these lands, the peasants often welcomed Ottoman rule.

The Ottoman way of life was based on warfare. Each spring, the sultan led his army out on a fresh campaign. After a summer spent fighting, the army returned home for the winter.

One reason for their success was the Ottomans' willingness to learn new ways of fighting. In Europe they learned how to use gunpowder. In the 1420s they began to build enormous bronze and iron siege cannon. Later, the janizaries took to using hand-held guns.

All power was held by the sultan. When he died, the throne passed to whichever of his sons was strong enough to seize it. The new sultan then executed his brothers and all their male children. Though brutal, this system led to strong central government.

This French painting shows the siege of Constantinople in 1453. In the foreground is Sultan Mehmed's camp. Behind him, you can see the giant siege cannon bombarding the city. You can also see the sultan's navy, blockading Constantinople from the sea, and a bridge made of barrels, built for transporting supplies.

Right *A Turkish painting of the Ottoman navy in the sixteenth century. For the first time, Christian Europe was threatened by a strong Muslim sea power.*

Below *The conquerors added minarets to the great church of Constantinople, Hagia Sophia, converting it into a mosque. The resulting building provided a model for later gigantic Ottoman mosques.*

The greatest conquests were carried out by three sultans, Mehmed the Conqueror, Selim the Grim and Suleiman the Magnificent. Mehmed earned his nickname by capturing Constantinople in 1453 – this had been the ambition of Muslim rulers for centuries. The city fell after a seven-week cannon bombardment. Mehmed then made it the Ottoman capital, Istanbul (a Greek word meaning 'in the city'). Its huge domed church, Hagia Sophia, became a mosque.

Between 1512 and 1517, Selim the Grim defeated the Ottomans' greatest Muslim rivals, the Mamluk sultans who ruled Egypt and Syria. These sultans were themselves from slave backgrounds – the word Mamluk means 'owned'. By

To the people of central Europe, the Ottoman Turk was a sort of bogeyman, a frightening and threatening figure who seemed invincible. Here is an extract from a popular German poem of 1494, Sebastian Brant's *The Ship of Fools*:

Suleiman the Magnificent, the most famous of the Ottoman sultans, campaigning in Hungary in the 1520s. This Turkish painting shows the janizaries and the siege cannon, as well as the great luxury of the sultan's travelling court.

**So strong the Turks have grown to be
They hold the ocean not alone,
The Danube too is now their own.
They make inroads where they will,
Bishoprics, churches suffer ill.
We perish sleeping one and all,
The wolf has come into the stall
And steals the Holy Church's sheep
The while the shepherd lies asleep.
For Europe's gates are open wide,
The foe encircles every side,
With sleep or rest he's not content,
On Christian blood alone he's bent.**
(Sebastian Brant (1457–1521),
The Ship of Fools)

Who do you think that the wolf, the sheep and the shepherd are meant to be?

the sixteenth century the power of the Mamluks had declined. Unlike the Ottomans, they were reluctant to use artillery, and were easily defeated.

The most famous sultan of all was Selim's son, Suleiman the Magnificent, who ruled from 1520 to 1566. Under Suleiman, the Ottomans conquered Hungary and even laid siege, unsuccessfully, to Vienna. They built a powerful navy which captured the island of Rhodes and attacked Malta and southern Italy. Suleiman also conquered Iraq and part of Persia. Although he spent so much time campaigning, Suleiman was also a patron of the arts and a maker of laws. He was known to Muslims as 'Suleiman the Lawgiver'.

The Scientists of Islam

Above *An astrolabe from Spain, engraved with Arabic and European letters. Such instruments were greatly valued by European navigators and astronomers.*

Between the ninth and fourteenth centuries many of the world's greatest scientists were Muslims. In mathematics, medicine, astronomy, chemistry and physics, Islam was far in advance of Europe. While Europe was going through a period known as the Dark Ages, the Muslims safeguarded, and built on, the knowledge of the Ancient world.

Some credit for Islamic science belongs to the caliph, al-Mamun. In 830, he founded a 'House of Wisdom' in Baghdad. This was a school, a library and a translation centre. Here the most important works by Greek, Persian and Indian scientists and philosophers were translated into Arabic. These works provided the foundation for Islamic science. Later, it was often through Arabic translations that Europeans came to know the great works of the Ancient Greeks – Galen's medical writings, Ptolemy's astronomy and geography, Euclid's geometry and Aristotle's philosophy.

The House of Wisdom also had an observatory for looking at the stars. Astronomy was very important to Muslims.

Right *Learning and religion were always closely connected in Islamic countries. This is the Shir-dar Madrasa, a great teaching mosque in Samarkand, now in the USSR.*

A Muslim astronomer plots the position of a comet using an instrument called a quadrant. Like the astrolabe, the quadrant was used for astronomy and navigation.

The Arabs had used the stars to guide them as they travelled the desert. Moreover, Muslims would look at the stars to work out the direction of Mecca, the direction in which to pray. Like the Greeks, the Muslims also believed in astrology; they thought that the stars influenced their lives. Today we still call many stars by their Arabic names, for example Betelgeuse (which means 'shoulder of the giant').

The most important tool for astronomy was the astrolabe. This was a Greek invention that the Muslims improved. It was a flat metal disc with a pointer that moved round. By directing the pointer at a star or at the sun, the observer could then read on the astrolabe how high the star or the sun was above the horizon. With this information Muslims could tell the exact time of day or night and they would then know the right time to pray. In this way, religious practice gave a motive for the development of science.

The astrolabe was also used for navigation at sea. The position of the sun or the Pole Star, shown on the astrolabe, would tell a sailor how far to the north or south he was. Mathematicians used the astrolabe to work out the distance around the earth. They did so at a time when most Europeans thought that the world was flat.

A Spanish painting of chess, a game invented in India and introduced to Europe by Muslims. The word 'checkmate' is thought to come from the Persian phrase, 'shah mat' which means 'the king is lost'.

Such calculations were made possible by Arabic numerals, the numbers which the Muslims brought to the West from India and which we still use. Previously, numbers had been written out as strings of letters, each one representing a different rank (ones, tens, hundreds, etc.). Big numbers were shown by adding extra letters. The Arabic system used a symbol for individual numbers (1, 2, 3, etc.). The number's rank was shown by its place. This system needed a symbol for an empty place, and so the zero was invented. Arabic numerals were much more efficient: for example, the Roman number LXXXVIII could now be written as 88.

The first book on these new numbers was written by al-Khwarizmi, one of the scholars who worked for Caliph al-Mamun. He also wrote the first book on algebra, the type of mathematics that uses letters or symbols to solve problems (algebra is itself an Arabic word, *al-jabr* meaning 'joining together' or 'restoration'). These books were used by Europeans as their main mathematics textbooks until the sixteenth century.

The Muslims were also fascinated by chemistry, a word which comes from the Arabic *al-kimiya*, or alchemy. Alchemy means to change something from one substance into another. The Muslim alchemists tried to change ordinary metals into gold. They never succeeded in making gold but they did develop many of the methods still used by chemists. Many chemical terms, such as alkali, alcohol, alembic and amalgam, are Arabic words.

We owe the greatest debt of all to Islamic medicine, in particular to the work of two Persians, ar-Razi (865–925) and Ibn Sina (980–1037). They became famous in Europe where they were known as Rhazes and Avicenna. Each wrote an important encyclopaedia of medicine, based on wide reading and practical experience of treating people. Avicenna's enormous work became the main guide to medicine in European universities. Rhazes also wrote an important book on smallpox, giving the first description of the disease's symptoms.

The Persians were rivalled by the scholars of Muslim Spain. The greatest Spanish medical writer was Ibn Rushd (1126–98), known in Europe as Averroes. However, he was most famous not for medicine, but for his writings on philosophy. Unlike modern scientists, the Muslims did not specialize in one subject: Avicenna wrote books on philosophy,

Muslim doctors were much more advanced than European doctors. Usama ibn Munquidh (1095–1188) included in his memoirs an account from an Arab doctor who treated Europeans, or Franks, in Syria:

They took me to see a sick woman. I ordered a cleansing and refreshing diet for her. Then a Frankish doctor appeared, saying, 'This man has no idea how to cure people!' He examined the woman and said, 'She has a devil in her head who is in love with her. Cut her hair off!' This was done, and she went back to eating her usual Frankish food, garlic and mustard which made her illness worse. 'The devil has got into her brain,' pronounced the doctor. He took a razor and cut a cross on her head, peeling back the skin so that the skull was laid bare. This he rubbed with salt. The woman died instantly. Thereupon I asked them if they had any further need of me, and as they had none I came away, having learnt medical methods that I never knew before.

(Quoted by Usama ibn Munquidh, *Memoirs*)

Which doctor would you rather see if you were ill and which doctor's methods were better? Why?

A thirteenth-century Italian book on surgery. Compared to Islamic countries, European medicine was very crude. Unlike the surgeon shown here, many Muslims used anaesthetics to send their patients to sleep before they operated on them.

astronomy, law, mathematics, physics and religion, as well as some poetry. Rhazes wrote on chemistry, astronomy and religion. The greatest Persian mathematician, Omar Khayyam, who died in 1131, was also an astronomer and a physicist. Yet in Europe, he is remembered for his poetry.

It was often through contact with Muslims (in Spain, the Middle East and Sicily) that Europeans were introduced to scientific knowledge. It was also the Muslims who introduced Europe to the technology of India and China. So many of the things we take for granted today, including the knowledge to make the paper on which this book is printed, have come to us from the civilization of Islam.

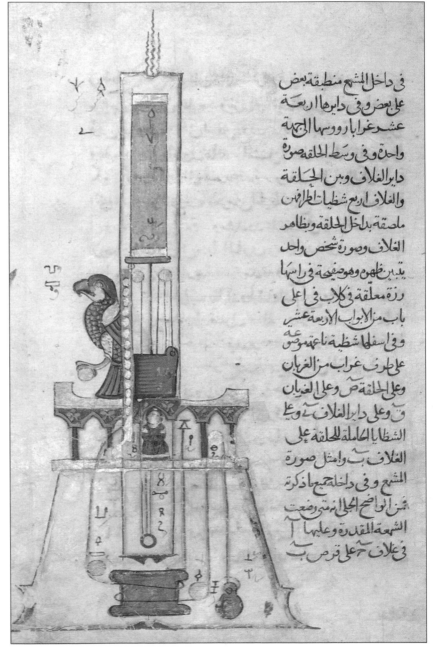

A candle-powered clock, from a book of mechanical devices, written by an inventor called al-Jaziri between 1181 and 1206. Each hour, as the candle burned down, a golden ball was released from the carved falcon's claw; a door opened and a tiny figure emerged.

Timeline

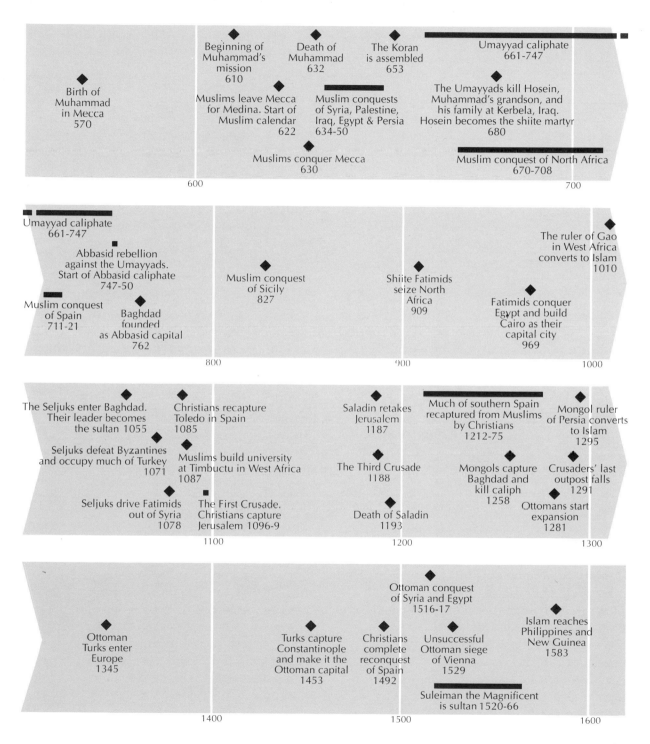

Birth of
Muhammad
in Mecca
570

Beginning of
Muhammad's
mission
610

Muslims leave Mecca
for Medina. Start of
Muslim calendar
622

Muslims conquer Mecca
630

Death of
Muhammad
632

Muslim conquests
of Syria, Palestine,
Iraq, Egypt & Persia
634-50

The Koran
is assembled
653

Umayyad caliphate
661-747

The Umayyads kill Hosein,
Muhammad's grandson, and
his family at Kerbela, Iraq.
Hosein becomes the shiite martyr
680

Muslim conquest of North Africa
670-708

600

700

Umayyad caliphate
661-747

Abbasid rebellion
against the Umayyads.
Start of Abbasid caliphate
747-50

Muslim conquest
of Spain
711-21

Baghdad
founded
as Abbasid capital
762

Muslim conquest
of Sicily
827

Shiite Fatimids
seize North
Africa
909

Fatimids conquer
Egypt and build
Cairo as their
capital city
969

The ruler of Gao
in West Africa
converts to Islam
1010

800

900

1000

The Seljuks enter Baghdad.
Their leader becomes
the sultan 1055

Seljuks defeat Byzantines
and occupy much of Turkey
1071

Seljuks drive Fatimids
out of Syria
1078

Christians recapture
Toledo in Spain
1085

Muslims build university
at Timbuctu in West Africa
1087

The First Crusade.
Christians capture
Jerusalem 1096-9

Saladin retakes
Jerusalem
1187

The Third Crusade
1188

Death of Saladin
1193

Much of southern Spain
recaptured from Muslims
by Christians
1212-75

Mongols capture
Baghdad and
kill caliph
1258

Crusaders' last
outpost falls
1291

Ottomans start
expansion
1281

Mongol ruler
of Persia converts
to Islam
1295

1100

1200

1300

Ottoman
Turks enter
Europe
1345

Turks capture
Constantinople
and make it the
Ottoman capital
1453

Christians
complete
reconquest
of Spain
1492

Ottoman conquest
of Syria and Egypt
1516-17

Unsuccessful
Ottoman siege
of Vienna
1529

Suleiman the Magnificent
is sultan 1520-66

Islam reaches
Philippines and
New Guinea
1583

1400

1500

1600

45

Glossary

Arabic words are spelt in a variety of ways in English. For example, in other books you may come across 'Koran' as 'Qu'ran' and *hijra* spelt as *'hegira'*. We have aimed to use the simplest and most common spellings.

Abbasids A dynasty of caliphs that ruled from 750 to 1258.

Allah The Arabic name for God.

Astrolabe A scientific instrument for measuring the position of the stars and the sun. It was used to tell the time and for navigation.

Ayyubids A dynasty of sultans that ruled Egypt and Syria from 1171 to 1260.

Bedouin Arabic name for nomads, desert tribes who herded flocks.

Berbers The native people of North Africa.

Byzantine Empire A Christian empire ruled by the Greeks of Constantinople. It governed Turkey, Syria and Egypt before these lands were conquered by Muslims.

Caliph Title of the supreme ruler of Islam. It means both the 'successor' and 'deputy' of Muhammad.

Dhow An Arab trading boat with a triangular sail.

Dinar Arab gold coin, modelled on the Roman denarius.

Dirham Arab silver coin, modelled on the Greek drachma.

Fatimids A shiite dynasty of caliphs that ruled Egypt from the tenth to the twelfth centuries.

Franks The people of France. The name given by Muslims to all Western Europeans.

Ghazi A warrior in the Muslim holy war.

Hajj The pilgrimage to Mecca and Medina which every Muslim is supposed to make.

Hanif An Arab who believed in a single god before the teachings of Muhammad.

Hijra Muhammad's migration from Mecca to Medina in 622. It marks the start of the Muslim calendar.

Imam A leader. The shiite name for their claimant to the supreme leadership of Islam. Also a prayer leader in a mosque.

Janizary An Ottoman infantryman, recruited from Christian slave boys taken from Greece and the Balkans.

Jihad Literally 'striving' or 'effort'. The Muslim holy war against unbelievers.

Kaaba Cube-shaped temple in Mecca, supposedly built by the prophet Abraham. The holiest place in Islam.

Koran 'Recitation', the title of the Muslim holy book. Muslims believe that it contains messages given by God to Muhammad.

Mahdi The 'divinely-guided one'. The name given to the man from the family of Muhammad who, according to some Muslims, will one day bring justice and plenty to the earth.

Mamluk Means 'owned' i.e. 'slaves'. Name given to the sultans of slave background who ruled Egypt and Syria from 1250 to 1517.

Mihrab Niche in the wall of a mosque showing the direction of Mecca, the direction of prayer.

Minaret The tower of a mosque.

Mongols A warlike race from central Asia. In the thirteenth century, the Mongols conquered many Islamic lands. They were later converted to Islam.

Mosque A Muslim building designed for prayer.

Muezzin A man who calls Muslims to prayer.

Ottomans A Turkish tribe, named after their founder, Osman. Between the fourteenth and the seventeenth centuries, the Ottomans conquered the Middle East and a large part of Eastern Europe.

Outremer The land beyond the sea. The name of Christian states set up by the

Crusaders in the lands they conquered.

Quraish The Arab tribe that lived in Mecca.

Ramadan The ninth Muslim month, set aside for fasting.

Saracen A Greek name for the Arabs. It was used by the Crusaders to refer to all Muslims.

Seljuk A Turkish tribe, named after their founder, Seljuk. They conquered Persia, Iraq, Turkey, Syria and Palestine in the eleventh century.

Sharia The holy law of Islam, based on the Koran, and on the example of Muhammad.

Shiites Muslims who belong to the shia, or party, of Ali and who believed that the caliph should be a descendant of Muhammad through his son-in-law, Ali.

Sipahi An Ottoman cavalryman.

Sultan Arabic title meaning 'power' or 'ruler'. It was used, particularly by Turks, to mean a political and military leader.

Sunni A Muslim belonging to the majority group in Islam, opposed to the shiites.

Turks A nomadic race from Central Asia which eventually settled in the land that is now called Turkey. After the eleventh century, Turks provided a majority of Muslim leaders and soldiers.

Umayyads A dynasty of caliphs which ruled Islam from 661 to 750.

Vizier 'Helper', a high officer of state. Under the Abbasids, the vizier was in charge of day-to-day government. Each Ottoman sultan had several viziers.

Zoroastrian A follower of the ancient religion of Persia. Like Islam, Zoroastrianism was based on the belief in a single god, announced by a prophet Zoroaster. It was tolerated by Islam.

Books to Read

A Latif al Hoad, *Islam*, Wayland, 1986

Maryam Davis, *The Life of Muhammad*, Wayland, 1987

Antony Kamm, *The Story of Islam*, Dinosaur Publications, 1976

Anton Powell, *The Rise of Islam* (Great Civilizations) Longman, 1979

Index

Picture Acknowledgements

The publisher and author wish to thank the following: C. M. Dixon 16, 17, 20 (both), 23, 27, 34, 40 (both); Mary Evans 15; Werner Forman Archives 4, 7, 12, 13 (top), 18, 24, 47; Sonia Halliday 19, 21, 24, 26, 30, 35, 38, 39; Michael Holford, cover, 6 (right), 8, 29, 42; Hutchison Picture Library 6 (left); Mansell Collection 9; Ronald Sheridan 14, 28. All other pictures are in the Wayland Picture Library. Artwork is by Peter Bull.